zendoodle coloring

Crazy Kittens

Other great books in the series
zendoodle coloring

Baby Animals

Baby Animal Safari

Bad Dog!

Big Picture: Birds and Butterflies

Big Picture: Calming Gardens

Big Picture: Mindful Inspirations

Big Picture: Magnificent Animals

Caring Thoughts

Celestial Wonders

Chubby Cherubs

Cozy Cats

Creative Reflections

Cuddle Bugs

Fantastic Creatures

Funky Monkeys

Happy Thoughts

Hopeful Inspirations

Inspirations for Moms

Into the Forest

Loving Expressions

Magical Fairies

Magical Mermaid Kitties

Majestic Dragons

Merkitties in Love

Nice Kitty!

Playful Puppies

Puppy Love

Sparkly Unicorns

Tranquil Gardens

Tropical Paradise

Under the Sea

Uplifting Inspirations

Winter Wonderland

Wise Owls

zendoodle coloring

Crazy Kittens

Fun-Loving Fur Babies to Color and Display

illustrations by

Jodi Best

CASTLE POINT BOOKS

NEW YORK

ZENDOODLE COLORING: CRAZY KITTENS.
Copyright © 2019 by St. Martin's Press. All rights reserved.
Printed in the United States of America. For information, address
St. Martin's Press, 175 Fifth Avenue, New York, N.Y. 10010.

www.stmartins.com
www.castlepointbooks.com

The Castle Point Books trademark is owned by Castle Point Publishing, LLC.
Castle Point books are published and distributed by St. Martin's Press.

ISBN 978-1-250-20242-0 (trade paperback)

Our books may be purchased in bulk for promotional, educational, or business use.
Please contact your local bookseller or the Macmillan Corporate and Premium
Sales Department at 1-800-221-7945, extension 5442, or by email
at MacmillanSpecialMarkets@macmillan.com.

First Edition: February 2019

10 9 8 7 6 5 4 3 2 1

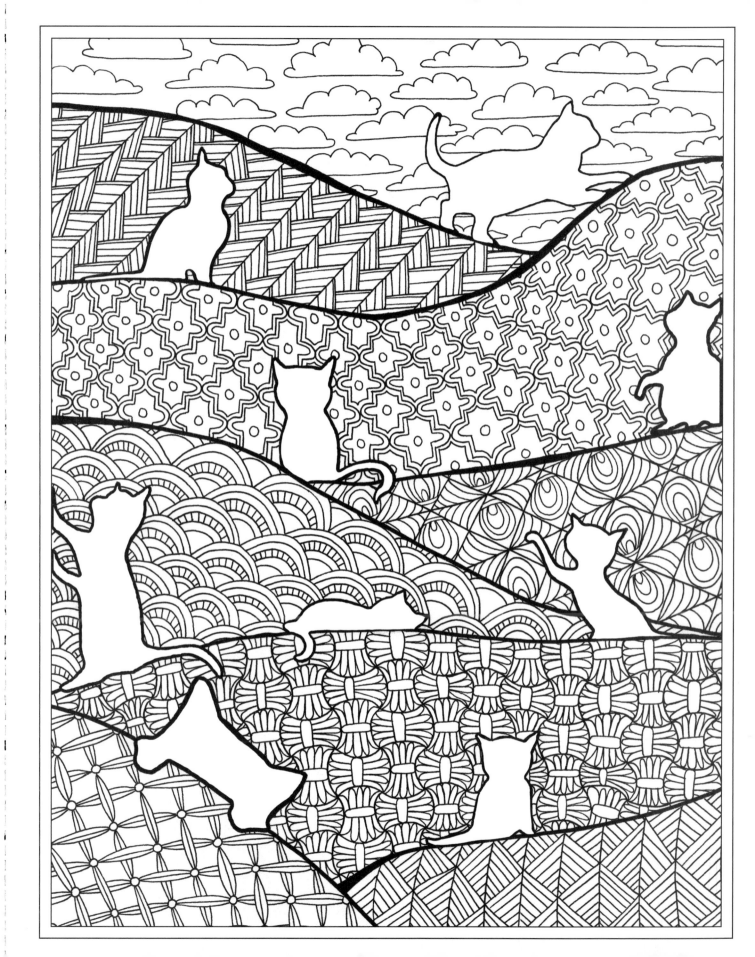

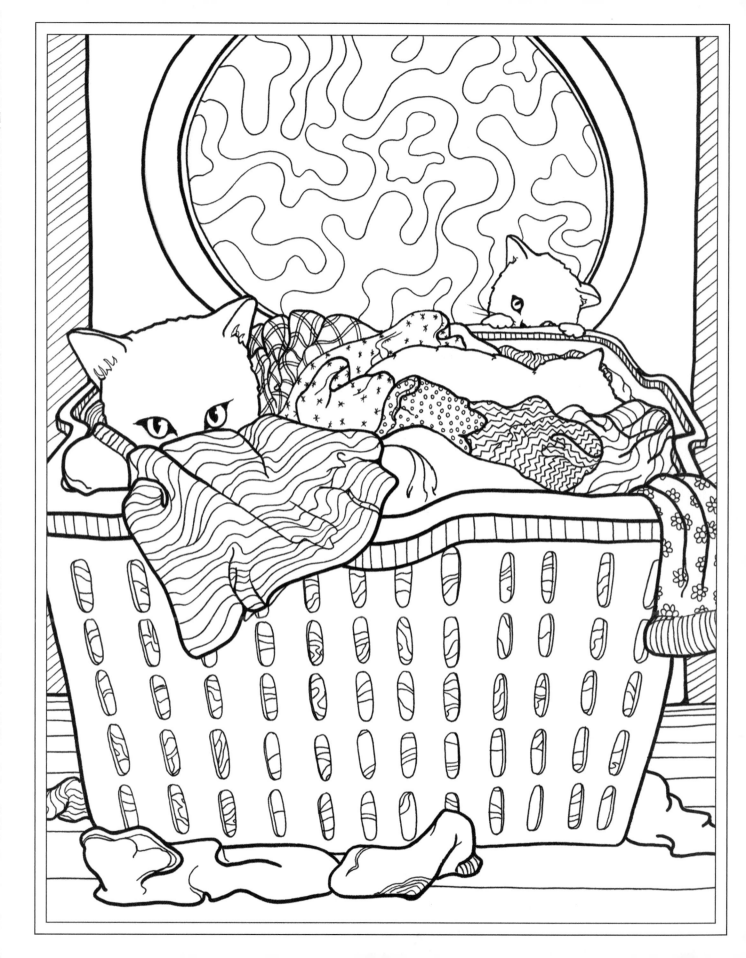

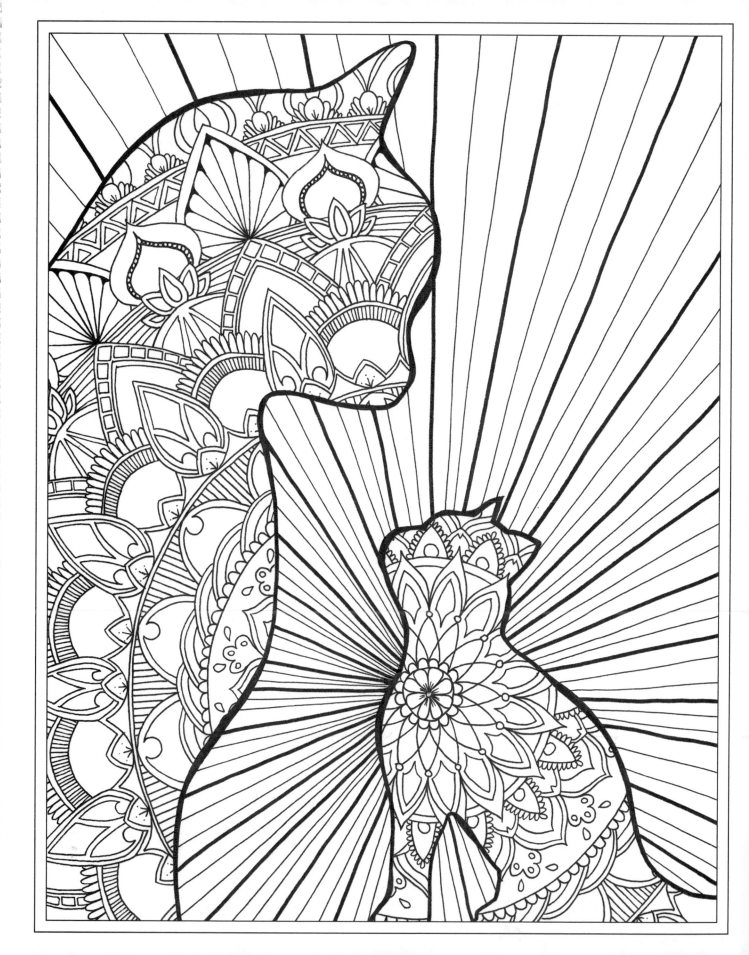

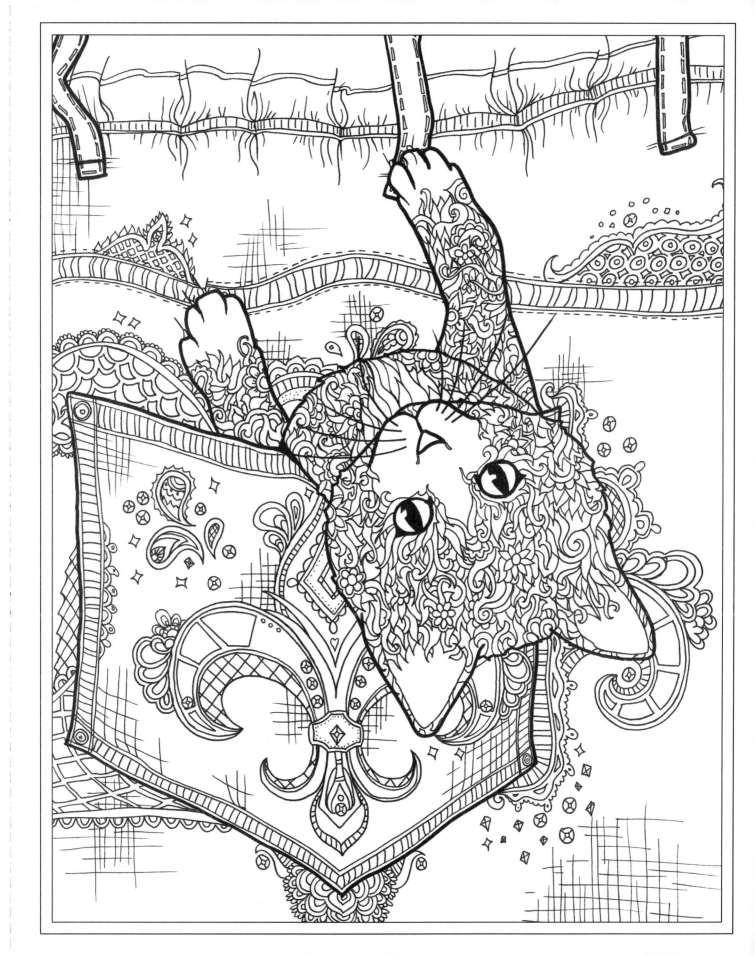

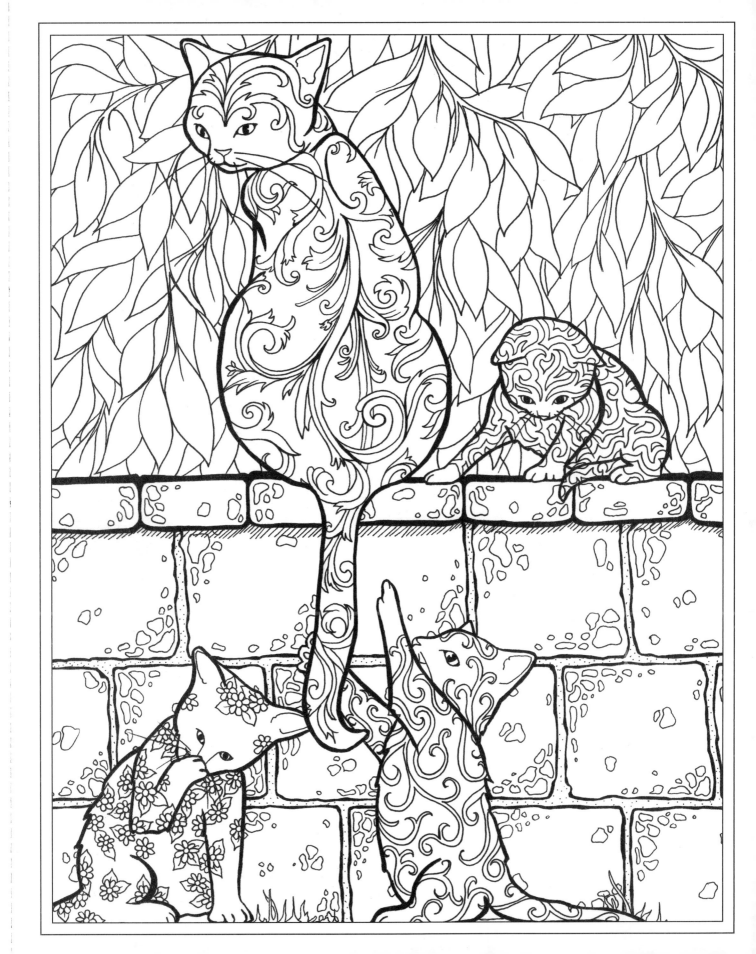

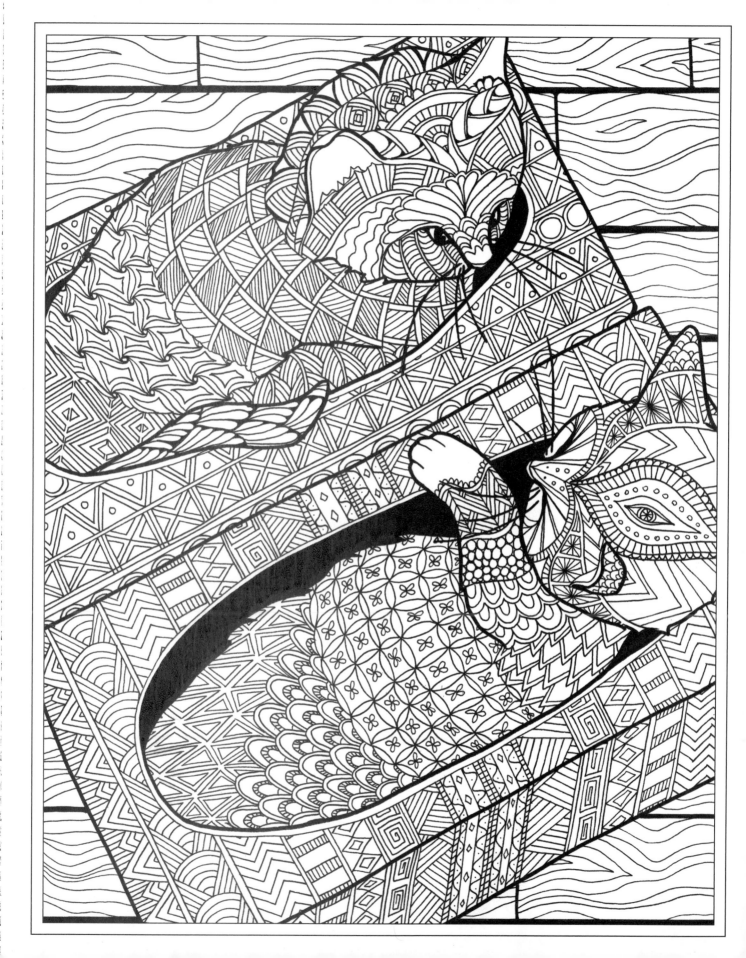

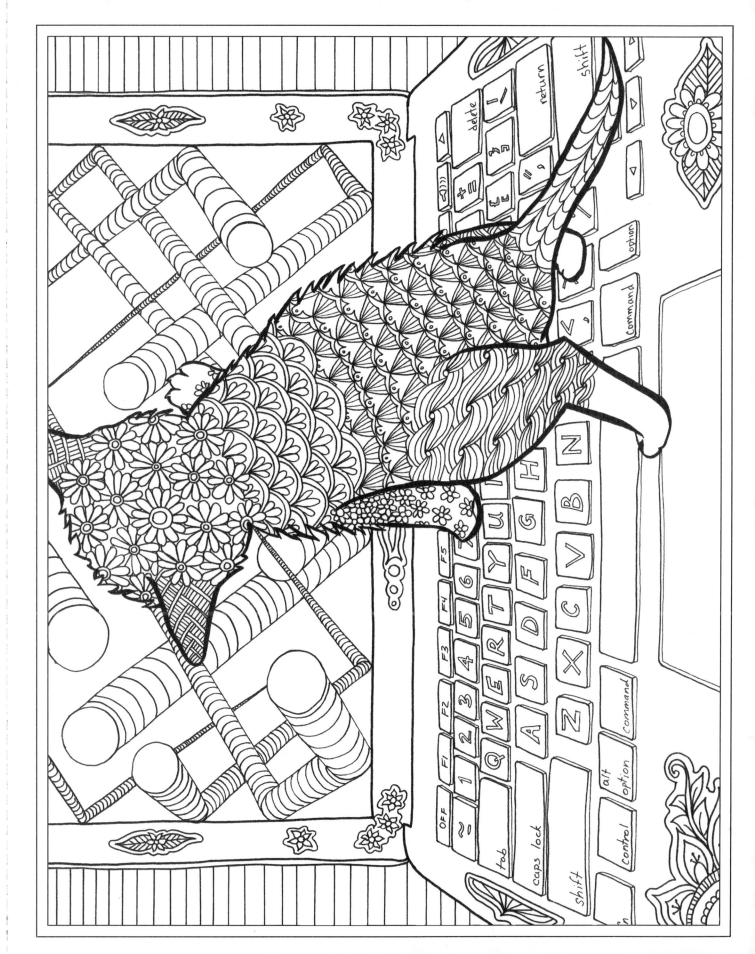